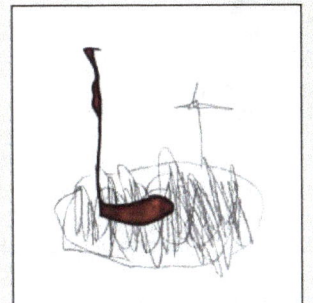 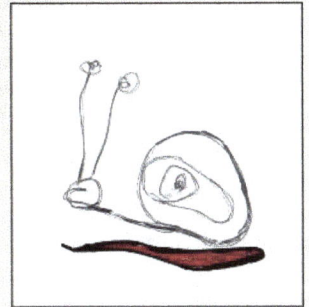

ONE SOCK IN A BATH
&
THE CEILING SNAIL

Tina Cooper

First published in Great Britain, 2025 by C H Press, a division of Creative Hats.

Copyright © Tina Cooper, 2025

The moral rights of Tina Cooper to be identified as author of this work has been asserted by them in accordance with the © Copyright, Design and Patent Act, 1988.

All rights reserved. No part of this publication may be reproduced, stored in a retrieval system, or transmitted in any form or by any means, electronic, mechanical, photocopying, recording or otherwise without the prior written permission of the publishers. This book may not be lent, hired out, resold, or otherwise disposed of by way of trade in any form of binding or cover other than that in which it is published, without the prior consent of the publishers.

Cover design using original Art – *Hattie Cooper and William Cooper*

ONE SOCK IN A BATH

&

THE CEILING SNAIL

For Squidge & Boom

I love you more than I thought it possible to love anyone.

Also I'm hungry and I need a wee.

love mum
— x —

Recently, years ago, some people, half a dozen friends and family, told me I should write a book but I had no idea what to write about. I decided to ask the kids, this is for them after all, and they gave me a list. This list contains such gems as jam tarts, dinosaurs, teeth and others. I then threw in a few old Facebook posts and some photos to pad it out. Many, many, many years from now, when I'm as dead as a dead thing, they will find a copy of this book at the back of a drawer and have a quick flick through before they donate it. I hope that whoever ends up reading it enjoys it as much as they might have.

People
~~Places~~ PLACES
Things
Food
Family
Friends
Holidays
Money
Feelings
The tooth fairy

Jam tarts
Dinosaurs ✓
Dogs + Pets ✓
Polution
Adventures
Children
Christmas
Halloween
That's it isn't it?
Computers

The Original List

One Sock and Ceiling Snail List

People	7
Things	16
Family	18
Holidays	24
Feelings	28
Jam Tarts	32
Dogs and Pets	35
Adventures	41
Christmas	46
That's it isn't it?	52
Places	57
Food	63
Friends	67
Money	71
The Tooth Fairy	75
Dinosaurs	82
Pollution	87
Children	93
Halloween	97
Computers	101

People

People are fascinating. I love 'em, most of 'em, some of them are arses, but all have stories to tell and I do love a good story. Some leave a lasting impression, others not so much. Some will impart extraordinary wisdom, some will make you smile long after they are out of your life and some will irritate the living daylights out of you, but many will leave a mark, a small mark perhaps but a mark nonetheless.

For example, the little old lady who came into the bakery every Friday and pointed directly at the fresh cream jam donuts.

"When those come in, could you save me four please?" she would say.

The first time she asked I tried to explain that we had them in, that she was in fact looking at them, but she just repeated her request. I placed four in a box and she thanked me and told me she would pop back later once they'd been delivered to the shop.

How marvelous. I looked forward to Fridays. Fridays made me chuckle.

Then there was the man who told me he'd been diagnosed with MS years before.

Fearing the worst he asked his doctor, "what do I do now?"

His doctor replied, "as much as you can for as long as you can."

I've kept this nugget as it's sound advice for anyone under any circumstances.

Then there was that lady in Bedford who had fallen over. I, a strapping 17-year-old, rushed over to help her.

"Fuck off!" she said.

This one stayed with me because this is the moment I realised not everybody wants help. I do but not everybody does. If you see me face down on the pavement do feel free to hoy me up. Thank you.

(just Googled hoy... that might not mean what I think it means but it's staying because I like it)

So. People.

They come in all shapes, sizes, and varieties, which is what makes them all the more interesting. I have been known to quiz new people to within an inch of their patience and then do it again because I forget everything almost instantly. This is why I can read a book or watch a film more than once and the ending is always a surprise.

The trick in life is to find your people. Your kindred spirits, your favorites, your happy place in those around you. This is not easy, it takes time and your people may change as you do, thus finding your people is an ongoing endeavor.

Your first people are easier to find as they are given to you.

Here they are, these are yours, your parents. Now, just to make things interesting, parents come in various forms. They might be yours by birth, one might be a stepparent or both could be yours by adoption but, however you come by them, they are now your people for the foreseeable. You don't get to choose these people so you kinda have to make the best of whoever you find yourself with.

If you're lucky, like me, your parents will be kind and funny and your early years will be joyous, full of biscuits and trips to the seaside. Some might not be so lucky but one thing is for sure, these people will help form the person you will become. Your first people will be rather influential, good or bad.

As you move along the bus of life you will get to choose your people. You might find that you're not very good at it at first but you will learn as you go along. Honest. Your people might be those with similar interests, they could be gamers, long distance runners or Trekkies or you could have nothing in common with them at all (for example The Husband and Me) but you'll tick along quite nicely anyway.

In your 20s you could have drinking and clubbing people then, once children enter the frame, you could have playground people. One or two drinking people might also be playground people but it's more likely that these two groups won't crossover as your drinking people might still be drinking and not yet playgrounding or they might just hate children and standing in a playground is their idea of hell on earth. Playground people will tell you when world book day is so keep these people close. They may also ask you to bake cookies for school, ignore these requests they are unnecessary, bakeries exist for a reason, do not entertain this nonsense, push these people away.

You might, one day, be diagnosed with a maddeningly frustrating illness and your doctor will send you to a group for people with said illness, these now become your people despite you never having been drunk or stood in a playground with any of them. These people do not know your drinking or playgrounding people but these people will understand, more than anyone else in the world, what it has taken for you to show up for that lunch date and that's what makes these people so blooming marvellous.

You will also pick up people as you wander from job to job. You could have Roger's Bakery People, Royal Mail People, Shuttleworth Swiss Garden People or Pharmacy People*. You could also collect a few bonus extra people when, in your 50s, you decide to go to college.

These are all my people, they float in and out of my life and your people might too but they all leave a little something behind. It might be a hilarious memory, a book you forgot to return or a recurring nightmare but a little something they will have left.

Your steadfast people will be your family, like it or not. You can try and shake them off by moving to a faraway land but your mum will still be your mum, your kids will still be your kids and so on, no amount of time or miles can change that.

My favourite people in the whole wide world are William and Hattie. I am at my happiest when stuck in a room with those two. Even though they ignore me nowadays, unless they are hungry or poorly, they are still my top choice of people to hang out with. A trip to a supermarket will be far more fun/expensive, a sit in the garden will be far more soothing and a moan over the dinner I've massacred will be far more annoying.

They just make everything more everything.

Whilst you're strolling the globe, picking up people along the way**, I wonder what sort of people you will be? One who doesn't want any help? One who will spread wisdom? Or one who will make others chuckle? I don't think any of us appreciate just how much we touch the lives of those around us. My dad was one who had no idea and was always surprised when someone thought highly of him. I've no idea why this was because he was a fabulous person but when one of his customers popped in to see how he was, after a trip to hospital, he welled up when he told me, "they didn't want anything, they just came to see me."

Have we helped along the way? Have we inadvertently made a person's day? Have we accidentally said something profoundly helpful at just the right moment to a person who was struggling?

Or, have we, at the very least, tried our very best not to hurt or hinder? Not doing a terrible thing is as good as doing a good thing surely?

I think it's always handy to remember that not everyone will like you. I made this mistake. I liked everyone and believed the same to be true of me but you can't please all of the people all of the time. Mother Teresa, who dedicated her life to charity, had haters and Hitler, one of history's most revolting, had a wife.

There really are no rules when it comes to choosing your people. It takes practice, there'll be some duds along the way, you might be someone's dud, but the duds help people choose their keepers.

I leave you with the wise words of The Doors...

People Are Strange.

*other jobs are available

**I once knew a man, Martin, who had been travelling the globe and bought himself a minibus which he affectionately called the Magic Bubble. As he made his way back to Old Blighty he'd pick people up along the way, the Magic Bubble was full by the time he made it home.

May 22nd, 2015

Driving home yesterday I said to William, "Look at all these people, where are they going, what jobs do they have, where do they live?"

He replied, "Don't know, don't care, it's none of our business"

Right. Yes. Of course. Just pondering is all.

Things

In this instance, baths.

I love a bath.

I love the sound of a bath running. I love testing the temperature. I like them hot. I love the feeling of the water enveloping me and taking any aches and pains away. I love the feeling of lightness. It's not quite the same as bobbing about in a swimming pool but it's the closest you can get whilst you're at home. I love letting the water out whilst I'm still in it and feeling myself get slowly weightier as if I'm coming back down to earth.

There's only one downside to a bath and that is that I hate them so much.

I never feel properly clean after a bath and they're so damn hot that I go completely lethargic, almost asleep, which can't be good when you're up to your neck in water. I then find it really hard to get out because I've gone all gormless, so I lay there until I am a prune or the water has gone cold or both.

Baths are the devil's work, sucking all life out of me until I am a mere husk. I end up a shrivelled version of myself. There's nothing behind the eyes except a vacancy for room to rent where my brain once sat.

I always end up in bed after a bath, so useless I become.

I loathe a bath.

March 20th 2015

I think it's a comfort thing? Children like to carry stuff from home as a reminder of a place safe and warm, things like a favourite cuddly toy or a blankie. William would carry a cigar but Hattie prefers a plastic cup full of plastic eggs.

Family

Well, this is a tricky one because we've lost a few members but still, I'll waffle on about family anyway because it's on the list.

Love them or loathe them you're stuck with them. Yes, you could move away or simply deny ever knowing them, but it matters not because you'll know who they are and they will lurk way back in the far distant recesses of your mind waiting to pop up unexpectedly to niggle or delight you.

Luckily, I love mine so they delight me... when they're not niggling me.

I'm obsessed with the children I didn't want, they are the only thing of note that I have done. At the time of writing, 9.45pm, they are 18 and 13 and just wonderful. The eldest is quiet and wise and soothing, the youngest is loud and chaotic and as mad as a barrel of biscuits. Both are my favorite people on earth.

I'm at my happiest when sat in a room with them. It's even more fun if they're arguing, my head will fall off one day such is the spinning of it. It's like Wimbledon but with fewer balls and cheaper strawberries. We three can sit in a silent room and giggle until I wee.

I'm hoping they never leave whilst simultaneously hoping that they do, so they have grand adventures to tell me all about. This is a lie I want them to stay with me forever.

I could bang on about how family isn't necessarily blood ties but a gaggle of your favourite people (or animals) that you have picked up along the way or I could just tell you about my family… yeah, I'll do that.

My mum. 73, crafty in both the shady sense and the making of things sense. Mum can knit, sew, make lace, build beautiful patchwork quilts and rattle out dishcloths that are far too delightful to wash your dishes with. She is diabetic but hasn't told her supermarket shop that small detail and buys family sized pies and trifles despite the fact that she lives alone. I know this because she lives in our garden now and her shopping is delivered to our house. Apparently the treats that arrive, the pies, trifles and Coke are for her grandchildren who don't eat pies, trifles or drink Coke. Mum buys me tubes of Smarties but I've got to be quick if a fancy any with a cup of tea. She is also far too generous for her own good, kind and funny as a funny thing.

The Husband. 48, kind, funny, likes a motorbike or 4 and does everything in a hurry or does nothing at all. He is good at accents and is a better cook than me but that's no great achievement as I am a terrible cook. He once baked a cream slice that could have been seen from space had anyone been looking. He has a lovely beard. If there's something we want to do or somewhere we want to go he will do his utmost to make it happen. He works hard for us and we all appreciate him very much. He's also really annoying and makes odd noises in his sleep that send me to the nearest sofa but on the whole he's a 9.25 out of 10.

William. 18, hilariously funny, wise beyond his years, anxious, autistic, will not share anything with anyone other than the dog and cannot be embarrassed. He is a hop skip and a jump from never leaving the house again since COVID showed him the way of the home learner/worker so I drag him anywhere I can. He'll come on a dog walk, I can get him on a dog walk, dog walks are the "anywhere I can". He loves the dog and tolerates the rest of us. His favourite thing to do is nothing or swimming. He is a lovely person but don't ask him if you look nice or if your new haircut suits you because he will tell you the truth whether you like it or not.

Hattie. 13, the kindest soul who ever lived, loud, doesn't listen to a word you say, loves dinosaurs and space, likes to "go for a drive" where she will play her music (Metallica, Black Sabbath, Motley Crue and Sir Mixalot) but not talk to you. She is easily embarrassed. As a toddler she was the most terrifying wee person, so much so that we stayed home between the ages of 2 and 3. We bought her a pretend kitchen from Ikea but she'd just lay across the top of it. We bought her a Little Tikes truck that she stood on the top of the one and only time she bothered with it. She was a danger to herself and others, we stayed home to protect the public. You're welcome.

Jackson. 8, hairy, smelly, grumpy, greedy. He hates everything and everyone who doesn't live at our address. He squeaks when he wants attention then, if he doesn't get it, he nudges me under my armpit with his nose. He eats everything that stands still long enough and will stare into your soul if you don't share.

Buddy. 7, ball of scruffy endless energy, full of joy. Buddy is the opposite of Jackson. When people visit we tell them to ignore our dog, he doesn't exist, then we offer them Buddy in way of an apology. He lives in the garden with my mum.

There are other members of the family but these are the ones I live with, the Daily Bunch. They're alright so I think I'll keep them.

*small edit

My brother. He wondered why he wasn't in this book. He had a point. I hadn't forgotten about him. I can't he's massive (in a tall, wide weight training kind of massive) it's just that he doesn't live with us. However, he did once so...

51. Has a glorious head of grey hair, just like myself, courtesy of our dad. Funny as a funny thing. Handy to know, he's a splendid carpenter whose talents are wasted. Once worked on the set build for one of the James Bond films, can't for the life of me remember which one, and his face was used as one of the baddies in a criminal data base for the film. I know right?! I'm related to a Bond star. Blink and you'll miss him but he's kindly given me the photographic proof. See attached blurry photo. It is him, honest.

March 7th, 2017

The dog has gone to work with Daddy, the house is so peaceful I could cry, in a good way. It is so quiet that I've had a moment to remember this morning's nonsense.

I climbed into bed with Harriet to gently annoy her awake, she rolls towards me and says, "Pretend you can't catch me because your arms are too small."

So, as any good mother would, I went all T-Rex on her, she loved it.

At breakfast William asked me what I'd done to his crumpets. "They're not cooked properly and why did you put so much jam on them?"

"Because I'm an arsehole," I say.

He wandered off to get himself a bowl of shreddies, he was not amused.

On the walk to school Harriet pondered her recent name change.

"Some of the teachers still call me Hattie"

I explained that some of us are finding it tricky to remember but that we'll get the hang of it.

"When I'm older I'm not going to be Harriet or Hattie, I'm going to be Sally."

Of course she is.

Holidays

Chapel St Leonards

We'd all, Nanny, Pops, The Husband, William, Hattie and I, gone off for the day to look at holiday chalets in Chapel St Leonards. We looked at many and picked one on the Eastfield's site a few miles up the road.

There was nothing on the site, no shop or pub promising entertainment, nothing. But. It was just over the road from the sea and, just over the road was a cafe, so all was well.

For reasons still unknown it took almost a year to complete on this wee holiday house with no chain, but we were thrilled when the day finally arrived to pick up the keys.

It had been shut a long time, we could tell by the smell of damp and the coldness of the beds but still, we loved it.

The best thing about it was that it was ours, we could go whenever we wanted for as long as we wanted and we wanted to go all the time.

A damp aroma would greet us whenever we arrived but would soon fade after opening all the windows, and the cold bed situation was easily fixed with an electric blanket on each. With every visit we'd leave more of our belongings, board games, paper and colouring pencils, toothbrushes, Nutella and tea bags, all the essentials. It was like going home but with less to do.

We didn't cook at Chapel St Leonards. Our first stop was always the local shop for supplies, and we'd make toast and sandwiches, eat biscuits and crips, and laze about for days on end.

We were so close to the beach that we could be down there at 5am with our dog who refused to poo anywhere else, then be back in time for breakfast. Back to the beach for ice creams and sandcastles, home in time for lunch. Sometimes we'd go to the beach after dark just because we could.

There was a telly that only worked when it wanted to, so we'd take DVDs to watch on repeat. We'd watch Pingu, Aquaman and The Croods with cups of tea, milkshakes and peanut M&Ms.

More often than not it would be just me and the kids and we'd barely move. The three of us would lay in the double bed with the electric blanket on high and natter about nothing in particular. Then we'd get snacks and natter some more. Many a happy hour was spent watching cake decorating videos on Pinterest or playing Connect 4.

About a mile along the coast was, and probably still is, the village with two amusement arcades, a gift shop, a fish and chip shop and a cafe.

There's not much at all in Chapel St Leonards but you must go immediately, if for no other reason than to do the nothing that is there.

July 16th, 2021

Excellent!

Cannot wait for the schools to close for the holidays. I am going to stock up on snacks then block all the exits. No germs in, none out. I'm just looking forward to not having to think about germs for six whole weeks. That and going to bed late, getting up late, not wondering why Hattie now hates school or why William still hates school, no more realising at 11pm that nobody has a uniform or that I've run out of bread. Nothing will matter, we will relax, be lazy, watch films, go for walks with the dog, play football with Hattie's new ball and lay on the grass staring up at the stars.

See you in September.

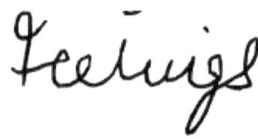

Feelings

It's love Jim but not as we know it.

When they are tiny and, let's be honest, utterly useless they need you for everything, right up until they are tall enough to reach the fridge door but, even then, they adore you.

You are the best thing to have ever lived. You're the funniest, coolest and most wonderful person and they want to be with you at all times. You have the answers to all of their questions and access to the internet for all those you do not. For example, how far is the moon from England and can penguins eat a Penguin. They want to paint, draw, watch Hey Dugee and water the garden with you. They will 'help' whenever they can by filling the dishwasher with clean plates from the cupboard then feeding the dog both their leftovers and their not-so-leftovers.

They are ever present.

You cannot escape them even if you want to and I did not. I was utterly obsessed from day one.

Then, one day, the inevitable happens and they realise you're just a human. You do not have superpowers after all. By this point they have probably fallen in love with one of their teachers, one who is particularly funny, one who calls them Dave instead of Hattie, and they will have even funnier friends.

Still, no need to panic just yet, they still like you very much. When they're hurt, sad or, more likely, hungry.

The hugs become less frequent. When you tell them you love them they say, "you're always saying that!" or worse "ok." They stop using full sentences and, in some cases, words. They retreat to their rooms and leave you unsure of what to do with yourself.

But, despite their best efforts at indifference, the love they have buried deep deep down in the far recesses of their little toe still shows itself, occasionally.

The foot of my daughter's bed ends at her door. When I go to bed I pop in and squeeze one of her feet. "Night Boom", I say. I can't see her because we painted her room a dark blue, including the ceiling, and added a space mural to one wall. She has a moon light that she never uses so it's like a cave in there.

One night I stuck my head in but couldn't find her feet. Then, out of the darkness appeared one black socked foot as she raised it high enough for me to squeeze.

"Night Mum."

That's love right there.

My son is a different kettle of biscuit because he has autism, so his love has always been nuanced to say the least. More obvious when he was younger because he needed me more than most but, now that he's 18, you have to really look for it.

One night I stuck my head into his room and said, "night Squidge."

Squidge nodded then turned back to his computer and his friends. A few minutes later, just as I was nodding off, a figure appeared at the end of my bed.

"What did you say Mum?"

"I said goodnight Squidge"

"I thought that's what you'd said, I just wanted to check. Night Mum."

That's love right there.

Your teenagers love you the same, it's just the way they show it has changed. Well, that's my theory and I'm sticking with it.

December 24th, 2021

It's not the snot that carries you off, it's the snotting they carry you off in or something.

Jam tarts

It is now widely known that jam tarts are the work of the devil, all sugar and no substance. It is also widely known that nobody cares because they are delicious. They are also one of a select few things that I can't screw up. Jam tarts, shepherds pie and, oddly, a roux.

I was once given a recipe for a three ingredient biscuit and still managed to make them inedible. Go me! But, the jam tart I can do. Well, in as much as they taste better than they look.

My mum used to make a big one with a twirly pastry lattice on top. We would inhale that bad boy, never lasted more than a few hours. Nowadays we tend to stick to a smaller version because diabetes etc.

So, the long and short of it is that jam tarts are marvellous in small doses.

May 12th, 2022

The Husband was home when I got back with the dog.

"Are you not working today?"

"Yeah, I'm waiting for an old lady, might nip to the garage for a coffee."

"We have coffee here."

"Yeah, but we don't have pastries"

"No, we don't have pastries"

Then, you're not going to believe this, he thought he was going to get coffee and pastries on his own!!

He's not. I'm in the van waiting.

Dogs & Pets

As an ex-postie who, at the time of leaving, held the office record for dog bites, I was horrified when the kids decided they wanted a dog.

"Hell no!" I was thinking as I asked The Husband.

He said no, hoorah, but the kids were relentless. Never have they wanted anything more. We took them to a nearby rescue centre because I believe in rehoming the unfortunate.

We were told that the best dog for children is the staffie and I agreed wholeheartedly. There was a staffie that lived in one of the flats I delivered to when I was a postie and he gave the best hugs. It was my favourite address on that round. The door would open and this absolute unit of a dog would bounce over and wrap his front legs around my waist as he grinned the biggest grin. I loved him.

The lady at the rescue centre wandered off to collect a suitable dog. He was five years old and very pleased to see us. The kids were not so chuffed as he jumped all over them. In their defence they weren't much taller than a staffie standing on his hind legs, so I understood their concern but was convinced they'd warm to him.

They did not warm to him.

Not to worry, they wandered off to sit on a bench with their dad whilst I walked the dog we weren't taking home. We'd been told we could take him for a walk and he appeared to be looking forward to it so off we went, the dog and I, for a walk in the woods. He found a stuffed toy monkey and couldn't have been happier. What a day he was having. I hope someone took him and his monkey and gave them both a loving home.

So. An older dog was too scary. A puppy then? Something small that would grow with them. We picked Jackson up whilst the kids were at school and couldn't wait for them to meet him.

Oh my word, they couldn't have hated him more.

William hid in the office and Hattie spent the rest of the day on the dining table. Both were terrified of the tiny beastie.

I couldn't hide of course. I'd drop the kids off at school and then head home to spend my days being continually bitten and wee'd upon. I hated the dog too. There were days that I didn't want to go home.

I watched youtube videos about stopping your dog biting you. Yelp. That was the advice, yelp because that's what your dog's siblings would do. To be honest it just seemed to fire him up, I'd yelp and he would savage me.

A stair gate saved the day. We put it on the kitchen door and every time the dog bit me I'd pick him up and pop him over the gate for a few seconds. It took a few goes but he got the message and we became friends of a sort.

Then magic happened.

I took him out for his first real walk, he had a blast.

By the time we got home he was worn out and promptly nodded off on the sofa. Along came my daughter, up till then she hadn't touched or spoken to the dog, she placed a towel over him, stroked his weary head and fell in love. She was closely followed by my son who now loves the dog more than anyone else to the point where he merely tolerates the rest of us.

The dog had stopped the nibbling and the jumping up with his pointy claws so was no longer frightening. I found that once the kids loved him, I loved him too.

Walking him was a pain though, other dogs were forever having a go at him and as an ex-postie who held the office record for dog bites I found this quite stressful. We decided to get the dog 'done' as we thought his enormous balls were offending other dogs.

When he came home from the vets, he was a little groggy but pleased to see us all.

"Has he had his balls taken away?" asked my daughter, then aged 5.

"Yes"

She bent down and patted him gently on the head.

"Good boy... Oh sorry, I mean good girl."

It turned out that his balls weren't offending anyone, perhaps it was just his face? I bumped into a wise old man on a walk one day, he'd had springers all his life, he told me not to worry as my dog would grow a pair. I secretly hoped not as we'd recently paid to have a pair removed.

The wise man was right, the dog did grow a metaphorical pair and stopped taking nonsense from other dogs. Word must have spread because nobody bothered him again. I would take the dog for a walk and just meet him back at the car later, he wouldn't bother anyone and anyone wouldn't bother him. Lovely.

Then covid happened.

My antisocial dog's Christmases all came at once. Nobody stopped to talk to his mum which meant he no longer had to tolerate mixing with other dogs, he could just get on with the job in hand, sniffing stuff. When covid calmed the fudge down and people returned to stopping and chatting the dog was over it and would tell anyone that would listen.

I paid a small fortune to have a dog behaviourist come to the house. The dog behaved impeccably and showed me up something rotten.

"You don't take a librarian to a rave," she said as she ran to the bank.

It was a small fortune well spent because it was then that I realised I shouldn't be protecting people from my dog, no, I should be protecting my dog from people and dogs and kids and the occasional rogue leaf.

We, the dog and I are much happier now. When he sees another dog he comes back to me to be popped on the lead and be given a treat. He is released when the not so dangerous danger has passed. Sadly this means I can't scrubble a new dog but hey ho, at least mine has stopped being an arse.

If you come to my house you will be told to ignore the dog, if you really need to scrubble a dog there is another living with my Mum in our garden and he loves everything and everybody so feel free to pop down there.

So, the dog and I walk alone and that's ok. Occasionally we meet another dog owner who doesn't give a damn that I've popped mine on a lead and will allow theirs to wander over. I will let them know that my dog isn't friendly, and my dog will show me up by not reacting at all convincing all dog walkers that it is in fact I who is the arse.

Anyhow. We now have a dog that hates everything and everyone, but we love the smelly, hairy, grumpy old boy. I hope we never bump into Ricky Gervais, he'd be so disappointed.

Adventures

Magic or witchcraft?

I'd never been knocked out before. I had been numbed for teeth reasons and blocked for c-section reasons, but I'd never been under a general anaesthetic and I was terrified.

I'm not sure what I was scared of, just the unknown I think. Oh and dying whilst out. I wondered if I should write letters to the kids. Perhaps I should write letters to the kids anyway? Perhaps this book will do? They're not going to read it whilst I'm alive, they'll shove it somewhere "safe" only to be seen again when they move house or have a spring clean.

I didn't write letters to the kids. Instead, I convinced myself I'd be fine, and I was fine. I think.

After meeting the anaesthetist and being told all the horrible things that could go wrong, including the highly unlikely chance of being awake throughout, I felt strangely calm. She was lovely and she made me laugh which was impressive under the circumstances.

I then met the surgeon who told me all the horrible things that could go wrong, including the highly unlikely chance of her perforating another, unrelated, organ and needing to fix it through my belly button. She too was lovely despite not making me laugh.

I then sat around for hours. I was number 4 on the afternoon list but I didn't know if that meant soon or not so soon. I settled down with a book and tried to forget that I was starving.

Soonish it was time to get changed into one of those hospital backless gowns, paper knickers and surgical stockings and I was nervous again. I needn't have been, I wasn't going anywhere yet.

At this point you're now in a room with other gowned patients.

You've seen them in the waiting room but now they are so close you can talk to them. We were all nervous and starving. It was good to have company.

My name was called by another lovely smiley nurse who apologised for the wait. Apparently, they'd had quite the day. I knew they had, I'd been watching the comings and goings and wondered how they were still standing let alone still smiling.

Once in the knocking out room I had to give up my shoes, the final task before being asked to "pop onto the bed" moments before they realised how short I was and went to get me a step.

A canula was put in and a blood pressure cuff fitted. A few of those sticky pads were added to my chest for monitoring purposes and I was asked what I was having done. I got a nod of approval from my surgeon when I got the right answer and felt strangely chuffed with myself.

Then a mask was popped over my face and I was told to breath and think about something, someone or somewhere lovely. I thought about swimming in Lake Garda.

"You'll start to feel lightheaded but keep your eyes open, so we know when you're asleep."

I didn't feel lightheaded. I was anything but lightheaded. I was staring up at the ceiling thinking that they'd better not take me into theatre whilst I'm still awake!

"Tina, how are you feeling?"

Wait. What?

"All done. You're in recovery."

I had a Google when I got home because I'm far too sensible to Google beforehand.

This is what an NHS website* said about anaesthetic...

> During a general anaesthetic, medications are used to send you to sleep. This means you're not aware of surgery and you won't move or feel pain while it's carried out. It's usually used for long operations or those that would otherwise be very painful.
>
> It's not clear exactly how general anaesthesia works. But, all anaesthetics interrupt the passage of signals along the nerves.

IT'S NOT CLEAR EXACTLY HOW IT WORKS!!!

Well, magic or witchcraft, it matters not.

I didn't feel a thing. I didn't know a thing.

All I can tell you is that the tuna sandwich and cup of tea I was given afterwards were the best tuna sandwich and cup of tea I'd ever tasted. Almost worth the worry and the wait.

I can also tell you that if you ever find yourself needing to be knocked out I highly recommend the Tavistock Ward at Bedford Hospital. Every member of staff I met were smashing and I hope I don't need to see any of them again any time soon.

Oh, does this qualify as an adventure? Perhaps I should have written about Lake Garda instead? It's beautiful there, well worth a visit.

*

November 14th, 2018

Sat waiting for a train. I'm off to London on my own! Something I would never have even considered before CBT. I'm cheating slightly as I'm meeting someone outside a florist in St Pancras, I know, it's all rather cloak and dagger. I'm feeling rather adventurous I must say.

I mean, I didn't buy the ticket or look at a timetable, I'm just going where I'm sent but still ...

The name is Cooper. Tina Cooper.

Christmas

I love Christmas, I always have. Even as fully grown adults my brother and I would set an alarm for 5am and wake our parents, we'd then make Mum go downstairs to check He'd been. Having now had children of my own I feel terrible, she must have been knackered. Mum now lives with us and is probably cross that I get my kids up at 7am and even then, I have to drag them out of bed just to holler "he's been."

The first Christmas I was with The Husband we'd been out, gotten rather tipsy, and decided that it would be a great idea to pick all his presents up from his house and walk them, whilst giggling, through the town to my parents' house just to make him get up at 5am with us. The Husband was thrilled. My parents had bought him a tent so he looked a tad shady carrying that at silly o'clock on a Christmas eve, it could have been a body albeit one wrapped in shiny paper.

When my son arrived, I still loved Christmas, he would sleep so Christmas eve was a breeze and the day itself an absolute joy. When my daughter arrived, it became a little harder, she didn't sleep so Christmas eve was a nightmare and the day itself an exhausting trudge. Still, we managed to keep on with the magic despite waiting until 1.00 am to be Santa.

One year we had snow, so I stayed up late to make reindeer tracks in the garden. In the morning, I waited to 'notice' them then called my then three-year-old boy.

"Look, there are tracks in the garden! This must be where they parked the sleigh."

"Oh yeah," said William with a dash of so what.

Marvelous, stayed up late for an 'oh yeah'. Never again.

Some years later I was told to take the kids outside on Christmas eve where they would be able to watch Santa fly over. We waited and lo and behold we did see Santa (a satellite) fly over. To top this off I then showed them Norad Tracks Santa.

"I believe in him now," said William.

"What do you mean now?"

"Now that I've seen him."

"But who did you think delivered the presents?"

He looked down at his feet.

"I thought it was you and Dad."

Oh. So the whole hoof prints in the snow was a waste of blooming time then.

Sadly, it was the very next year that he asked the question we parents dread more than any other.

"Mum, is Santa real?"

Fuuuuuuckkkk! I didn't know what to say so I panicked and ran downstairs to ask The Husband.

"He's just asked me about Santa, what shall I say?"

"Well you always said you'd never lie to them…"

Fuckety fuck fuck fuck!

"No, Santa isn't real, he was but now we just carry on the tradition of giving at Christmas. St Nicholas gave to the poor, he spread kindness and this is what we keep going today by giving gifts."

He was devastated, he'd only believed for one year and then it was all over.

I explained that we are all Santa, that he would now have the job of putting out the presents on Christmas eve to keep the magic going for his sister, he seemed pleased with this news. That was until Christmas eve.

There we were, surrounded by bags of presents that William and The Husband had collected from family and friends earlier in the day, waiting for the opportune moment. Hattie was then 4 so knew enough to try and stay awake for as long as possible, she'd just nodded off but we daren't move a muscle until we could be sure. The Husband, as is tradition, had long gone to bed. Myself and Santa's little helper held our breath.

"Ok William, let's do this."

William was emptying a bag, finding the names on the presents and popping them in the correct pile when he stopped sharp.

"Wait…"

I froze and waited.

"No, it was the dog."

We carried on.

"Wait…"

My nerves were shot. William was a terrible assistant, purely because his hearing was better than mine, so we had to stop for every noise, rustle or snore from upstairs.

"This is so stressful," William has said every Christmas eve since.

This year Hattie asked the question we parents dread more than any other.

"Mum, is Santa real?"

Oh no, I'd broken one heart, her dad could take this one.

As this is the 21st century she facetimed her dad who was downstairs at the time.

The Husband said this…

"Is Christmas real? Yes. St Nicholas used to give gifts and we carry on this tradition of spreading kindness at Christmas. Does a fat man in a red suit come down the chimney to deliver presents? No. Is that ok Hattie?"

"Yeah, that's fine. Thanks Dad."

I waited for the penny to drop but she couldn't have given less of a fig.

William arrived on the scene and we explained that she is now a Santa and she will help put the presents out on

Christmas eve. She seemed pleased with this news and wandered off to watch YouTube.

"William, you were more upset than your sister and you only believed in him for a year."

"I wasn't upset that Santa wasn't real, it was because you'd lied to me."

Of course, he's William, lying is big no no. I told him I was sorry and that Nanny made me do it. In fact, Nanny did make me do it, she knew I had trouble with Santa so each Christmas she would say "don't you tell him!" I haven't the words to express how happy I am that the charade is finally over.

I am now beside myself at the thought of Christmas. I'd never stopped loving it, it's just that I have struggled to fully enjoy it but this year, oh this year is going to be wonderful.

I'm going to go to bed before midnight. I haven't got to pretend to go to sleep whilst trying not to go to sleep. We can all put the presents out. Or, I could make them do it once I'm in bed for the full 'he's been' experience. They looked at me funny when I told them I would send them downstairs to check but I meant it.

I've got Christmas back.

December 25th, 2014

I love Christmas. Hattie woke up at 7am, asked "what's this all about?" then went back to bed.

That's it ain't it

So. This book came about because half a dozen friends told me I should write one after I'd penned a few mildly amusing Facebook statuses/stati/statusiz.

The Husband got wind of this and, like a dog with a donut, wouldn't leave it alone.

After some pondering, I remembered that I haven't a story in me. I'm not a JK Rowling or Doug whotsit of Hitchhikers fame. Alas, if it didn't happen, I cannot make it up.

The last time I saw my grandad he told me a joke about a camel getting its testicles squashed between two rocks. It was hilarious yet I couldn't recall the joke later. This sewed a small but perfectly formed seed.

I should write the things I think my kids might want to know once I'm gone. They'll know the obvious, I'm their mum, I married their dad, I was a postie etc etc but what about other stuff, the nonsense?

I asked them for chapter titles.

"What?" they replied in unison. "The book is for you, what do you want to know about?"

"People."

"Places."

"Christmas."

"Anything else?" I begged in desperation.

"That's about it isn't it?"

People, places and Christmas. That's it?

What about William's autism diagnosis or that day I took Hattie to Mad Hatters and she just ran around eating Mini Cheddars? Our trip to the Isle of Man in the camper when Hattie fell in love with a plug socket? Watching nanny's house being built in our garden after we lost Pops? I could have written about the funniest thing I ever said or about that time an old lady tried to kill me but no... people, places and Christmas.

I managed to get some more but it was like pulling teeth out of a stone. They were as uninterested then as they will be after the book is written but one day, when I'm long gone, they will find a copy lurking at the back of a drawer and have a quick flick through before popping it in the box marked for the charity shop.

December 22nd, 2023

Things I'm into at 52...

Candles.

Boiled sweets.

Jigsaws.

It's downhill all the way now isn't it?

Auntie Lynn

Tina Cooper
6 Feb 2021

A year ago this very day we were at the MK Theatre watching Peter Pan Goes Wrong without a care in the world. We had no idea of what was to come and, although it was a special night out, we completely took the whole thing for granted. I want to take things for granted again.

👍 Like　💬 Comment　📞 Send　↪ Share

Paul Cooper + 8

Lynn Evans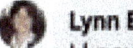
I know what you mean ....the freedom to go out wearing a skimpy bikini up Hamilton high street...I just took it for granted 😁 dont try to picture it because you'll get a headache...I was only in police custody for 24 hours and released with a caution...pop that in your book when you write it 😂
x

4y　Haha　Reply　　　　　2

Places

One of my favorite places is Shuttleworth. We were married here but that's not what I love about it. I loved coming here before and I have loved coming here since. So much in fact that I volunteered here until they caved and gave me a job.

At the time of writing, 2.15pm on the 15th July 2024, I'm here on my day off from being a drug dealer (deliverer of medication to the elderly, the infirm and the can't be arsed) to eat skin on fries with mayonnaise and write something, anything, for my book.

It's raining but weirdly warm. Most unpleasant to be honest but the chips here are amazing so I will suck it up.

When my daughter started nursery, I twigged pretty quickly that I was about to get very bored. Not one to bake cookies or do more housework than is absolutely necessary I decided I needed something to do. I decided to volunteer somewhere but where would I be happy going to work for free.

Enter stage right; the Swiss Garden at Shuttleworth.

I had to have an interview which came as a surprise, I thought I could just turn up. The Husband found this hilarious and quipped at how funny it would be if I didn't get the no money job. I did so he can poke it.

I was very nervous on my first day until one of the regular volunteers took the mickey out of me and I decided all would be well. I was right, all was well. Better than well in fact, I loved it.

I took it very seriously, if you say you're going to be at a place then at that place you should be, even when it is raining cats and dogs and you're going to be outside all morning. The particular morning I'm thinking of, myself and a fellow ex postie called Martin were clearing leaves. We laughed so hard at the ridiculousness of our damn good soaking that I almost wet myself. A good day for it because nobody would have noticed.

After a while my boss, Rosemary, asked if I'd like to be a garden steward. I wasn't sure, my kids were 11 and 6 at the time and they still bothered with me back then, so I was loathe to leave them as it was a weekend position. I said I'd think about it.

Fast forward a few weeks and Rosemary said we needed to pick a day for my training. It turned out that I had, quite accidentally, got myself a job, no thinking necessary.

My first day was the Father Christmas fly in day.

Yes, he flies into Shuttleworth, they have an airfield so it's a no brainer.

One of my duties was to guard Father Christmas during his lunch. I wasn't to let any eager children pass me. No problem, I can take out someone half the size of me, probably. I also had to radio his lunch order through to the restaurant. A ham sandwich and a diet coke in case you are wondering.

There I stood, at the door of the Swiss Cottage, radio in hand and red Christmas hat proudly perched upon my noggin feeling like private security to the Big Man.

All I could think about was how I couldn't put any washing on, I couldn't feed any of the children, I couldn't walk the dog and I couldn't hoover. I felt so relaxed that I almost fell over. For the first time in a long time, I had nothing to do except whatever I was told to do and, right there and then, I'd been told not to move.

This was going to be good for me. Thank you, Rosemary.

I've worked on weddings and Alice In Wonderland days. I've moved 30 plus yoga mats whilst nibbling on the left overs of their very tasty picnic. With their permission of course, I'm not a heathen. I've been on a mushroom hunt and I've hand printed Christmas wrapping paper. The best bit though is the airplanes.

The Swiss Garden is nestled behind one of the world's greatest collections of planes. It began as the private collection of Richard Shuttleworth and has grown over the years. They put on epic air shows in planes that are over 100 years old, one of which I had the pleasure of going up in. That was another thing I was told to do by my pal Fiona. At least I thought she was a pal until she asked the pilot if he had room for a passenger.

"Sure" he said "where do you live? We'll go over your house. Give your family a call and tell them to get ready to wave at you"

What the hell?!

I looked at Fiona and she just nodded so off I went.

I called the house and got my daughter.

"Hattie, get your dad and William and go to the garden. In a few minutes a silver plane will go over and I'm going to be in it. Get ready to wave"

"Dad and William?"

"Yes"

"Then what?"

"All of you go to the garden and look up"

"I can't see you"

"No, you won't, I'm not up there yet"

After losing the will to continue the conversation I just said I'd see her later.

"Ok Mum. Love you!"

Love you?

It was at this point that a man got out of the 130-year-old plane and manually spun the wooden propeller.

I was, by then, convinced that that was how I would die, in an ancient plane over my own garden whilst my family watched.

I didn't. The opposite in fact, I lived a little more that day.

Sometimes, whilst working in the garden, I can watch the air shows and ponder upon how lucky I am that I was bored at home and that Rosemary didn't take my screwed-up face as a no.

This isn't an advert but still, you must go to Shuttleworth immediately, if for no other reason than they cook a lovely chip.

May 14th, 2022

Sometimes you just need to spend a day at Shuttleworth with Eileen and a 99.

Eat the Frosties

I once had the pleasure of delivering medication to the elderly, the poorly and those that couldn't be arsed to collect it.

On the 31st of July 2024 I was heading to a see a chap that I delivered to each Wednesday. For the purposes of this wee story, you need to know that he had recently lost his wife.

On this particular day the road to his house was closed which meant I had to go around and up and through the neighbouring village to get to the other side of the roadblock. Upon arrival at the other side, I discovered that I still couldn't get to his house.

Never mind, it was a lovely day for a walk.

It was a stupidly hot day but on I trudged.

I walked past the roadblock only to discover that I could have reached his house via the original route but roadblocks never tell you how far you can go because they are placed there to ruin your day.

"Hello Sunshine," he said. "How are you?"

I regaled him with my tale of hot muggy woe.

"But, the good news is that I am walking off the bowl of Frosties I had this morning," I said trying to find the sweaty silver lining.

"I love Frosties, my nan used to get them in whenever I visited," he said.

"Me too. Close your eyes and you could be six years old again, but I think they're really bad for you."

"Yes, I think you're right but..." he gave me a look, "life is short, eat the Frosties."

January 4th, 2018

How many people does it take to eat ten of Mrs Bridges stem ginger and lemon luxury cookies? One, for fucks sake. ONE!

Friends

Well, that's more than a little vague. What do they mean? The TV series? My friends? Their friends? Old or new friends? Yet to be met friends?

According to Google a friend is 'a person with whom one has a bond of mutual affection, typically one exclusive of sexual or family relations'.

So anyone you like that you're not related to or sleeping with. Well that narrows it down.

It turns out that I have loads of friends then. I like many many people that I'm not sleeping with or related to. Of course I can't be sure that the feeling is mutual, not without asking and that's just weird.

In my experience you have different friends for different areas of your life. School friends. Friends you get drunk with. Work friends. Mum friends. College friends. ME?/CFS friends.

Sometimes they cross over. You might get drunk with a work friend or get drunk with an me/cfs friend. You could bump into a school friend whilst at work and wish you were drunk or, better still, dead.

Nothing worse than bumping into someone who last saw you when you were younger, thinner, carefree and less grey. It must come as such a shock to them.

I was once parked in a car park when I spotted a chap I hadn't seen in forever.

"Oh, we'll have to sit here for a bit," said I to William.

"Why?" he quite rightly asked.

"There's someone I used to know, and I don't want them to see me."

"Why?" he quite rightly asked again.

"Because I'm scruffy as fuck, my hair is completely grey and I'm twice the size I was back then."

"Him? That man there? You don't want to be seen by him?"

"No. Not today."

Then we watched as the blast from my past came closer. He had a full head of beautiful grey and a belly to rival Santas'. We then watched him struggle to get in his car.

"You didn't want to be seen by the man who can't get in his car because of his belly? Well that's silly, at least you can get in your car."

I think it was a compliment of sorts. What I'm trying, and probably failing, to say is that friends come in all shapes and sizes, some stick around while others do not. Many are your friends even when years have passed and you no longer look as you once did ... if they recognise you of course. No matter who, you will always share a time in space, shared memories of whatever it was you got up to together, memories that nobody can take away.

At least not until the menopause kicks in, then it's a minefield. I thought I'd seen someone I knew in Southwold.

It was Georgie Glen, the actress from Calendar Girls and Call The Midwife. I almost said hello, can you imagine the embarrassment.

I suppose this is where the, "bond of mutual affection" comes in.

I know Georgie Glen, from the telly, and I like her very much but she hasn't the foggiest idea who I am.

So, to make a short story long, friendships should be reciprocal, if not then you're just a stranger or, worse, a stalker.

October 15th, 2015

Friends huh, ain't they fab? I'm poorly and grumpy so a friend is making me her magic soup AND she's going to deliver. When she arrives, I'm going to love her and hug her and kiss her till I've passed it on because that's what friends do, they share.

Money

The main problem with money is that we haven't much of it. We go through phases of feeling quite comfortable and others of feeling quite not. The Husband is a self-employed electrician, so a regular wage is the stuff of daydreams, and I am between jobs having just lost one of the best jobs in the world. I also have me/cfs so I have limitations. I'm not sure what my next job will be, but I do know that I'd like one as it makes me feel like a useful member of society, even if only part time.

Sadly, we all have to have money, can't do much without it except breathe and if there was a way to monetise breathing then we would surely have to pay.

Sadlier still is that we have to pay for the boring stuff leaving very little to spend on the fun stuff. We have to pay for food, fuel, sanitary items, electric, gas, water, council tax and, rather oddly, the collection of our garden waste bin, a television license, Wi-Fi, Netflix and the like, clothes, shoes, medicines, dental appointments and car maintenance.

I'm not suggesting that we shouldn't pay for all of the above but, if we didn't, imagine what we could spend that money on. Holidays. Food but not the rubbish served at our house, rattled together by a woman who should really be able to cook as her grandad was a chef and once cooked for our dear Queen Elizabeth. No, I mean food in restaurants cooked by professionals like my grandad. Books. Quirky statues for the garden, I'm obsessed with an enormous steel T-rex that stands in a garden centre along the A1. A cleaner. Oooh, a driver. To be driven everywhere would be lovely. Stationary, pens, pencils and notebooks never to be written in and, most importantly, a wee house with a view of the ocean.

Of course, there are some things that are fun and free. Mooching about. For example, sitting in the garden with a cup of tea and a biscuit. Yes, I'm choosing to ignore the fact that I will have paid for the cup, the tea bag, the biscuit, the water and the electricity to warm it up. Going for a walk with the dog that we paid £500 for. Binge watching Reacher... on the television that we paid for with the license we pay for.

Oh dear, perhaps nothing is truly free.

On that cheery note...

I'm back to the breathing, enjoy it, it's all you have.

November 27th, 2016

Anybody else feel like emptying their bank of their last £13.50 and just getting in the car and driving? No? Just me then. See you when the money runs out... Hi there, what have you been up to whilst I was away?

The tooth fairy

... or serial killer?

I have a small heart shaped box that my son decorated at school when he was about 6ish. In this box I keep a bracelet he bought for me at a school Mother's Day sale, some blue wire that he'd twisted into a ring for me and a bunch of teeth. The kids' teeth, that is, not any old teeth.

Honest.

Only last week my daughter found the box. I know this because I found her wearing the bracelet.

"What else was in the box?"

"Teeth" she replied as if she hadn't just discovered the macabre in a beautifully decorated heart shaped box.

Inwardly I was relieved that the Tooth Fairy was no more. The days of creeping into their rooms in the wee small hours and swapping teeth for my hard earned were at an end. Hoo blooming rah.

Then...

Some days later, my daughter lost a tooth at the park, she casually handed it to me then carried on chewing on her sweets because nothing gets in the way of sweets. I popped it in my pocket ready for the Tooth Fairy.

On the way home I told her not to forget to pop it under her pillow when she went to bed.

"Ha," she chortled.

"What's so funny?"

"Nothing. Sometimes I just laugh randomly."

"No, you laughed at the Tooth Fairy. Why's that?"

I needed her to tell me the Tooth Fairy is nonsense because I wanted to avoid that panic at 2am when I would wake, sweating, and remember she hadn't been.

"Well, I was just thinking that you're the Tooth Fairy."

Yay!

"Right. So, do you want me to come into your room in the wee small hours and snaffle the tooth or shall I just put the money straight into your bank?"

"Wait. What? You are the Tooth Fairy? You've just ruined my childhood!"

Oh bugger!

"I'm going to tell everyone at school that there's no Tooth Fairy!"

"No, you misunderstood. It's not that there's no Tooth Fairy, I am the Tooth Fairy"

She wasn't listening.

"Oh... is that why there's so many teeth in the house?!"

Erm... why else?

Later I was relaying this conversation to my teenage son.

"So, what did she think when she found the teeth? If I'm not the Tooth Fairy then I must be a serial killer"

I laughed. He laughed.

Then he stopped.

"Wait. Why have you kept our teeth?" he asked in a manner that suggested he was displeased.

"I was going to put them in resin along with your umbilical cord clip and a lock of your hair. You know, like a Mini Museum* for my kids."

I thought he might vomit. He was mortified.

"That's the weirdest, most disgusting thing you've ever said."

I took a moment to ponder upon what other weird and disgusting things I have said that would make this the worst of them all.

"Why is it disgusting? Everyone keeps their kid's teeth."

I took another moment to wonder if other parents do, in fact, keep their kid's teeth or whether that was just my mum and now me because I'd grown up thinking that's just what happened to your teeth.

"No."

"Erm... yes."

"You've kept body parts!"

"Look, I didn't creep into your room and pull them from your head, they fell out, they were no longer needed."

"So if my arm fell off would you keep that?"

"Well..."

"I thought I knew you! And what's an umbilical cord?"

"That's the bit that joined you to me," I said, realizing immediately how disturbing that sounded.

"Wanna see it?"

"No... yes."

We wandered upstairs to find The Husband laying on the bed waiting for one of his feet to dry.

I explained the situation.

"Yeah, I heard. Look William, there's something you need to know about women, they will continually surprise you. Sometimes it will be a good surprise, sometimes it will be a bad surprise but what you need to learn is how to not change your expression. Just look them straight in the eye with a blank face and nod."

Undeterred I turned to Facebook.

> All you parents out there, what does your tooth fairy do with your kid's teeth?

Turns out many Mums keep their kid's teeth. One Mum has a full set. Got to admire that eh?

One keeps her son's teeth in a heart shaped box decorated by her son in primary school. Oh yes, the boys were in the same class and decorated the same box just for their Mum to have the same idea. I still think this is the best thing ever.

I was thrilled and rushed to tell my son.

"Mum. Just because lots of people do it doesn't make it normal. Lots of people are murderers, it's still not ok!"

I told him I'd throw the teeth away.**

*look them up, you won't regret it

** I am yet to throw the teeth away

October 20th, 2016

Hattie lost two teeth last night. I say lost, her dad pulled them out. The end result was that two teeth sat on a cupboard in her bedroom awaiting the arrival of the tooth fairy.

Funny how neither child would pop them under their pillow as is traditional.

Anyhoo. Hattie woke this morning to two shiny pound coins.

"Oh my God, she's been in my house. The fairy came to my house ... How did she get in?"

I told her it was magic but this didn't suit.

"Through the letterbox maybe?"

This was much better.

"I thought they were going to be chocolate coins but they're real coins," she said miserably.

You can please some folks some of the time but your children never.

Dinosaurs

My daughter has a thing about dinosaurs. As a wee person she would watch Jurassic anything, park, world, whatever scary many toothed creatures she could feast her mad little eyes on. At first, I thought it was because she knew I was terrified. I had told her about my visit to the cinema with my grandma.

My grandma had wanted to see Jurassic Park so we, Mum, Dad and I went with her. I'm yet to recover. I still have nightmares about the kitchen scene and the bit where my grandma couldn't find the wotsit you put your seatbelt into in the car so turned to me and said, "buckle me up Spotty."

Anyhow.

Whenever Hattie had a few moments or was off school poorly we would have to watch a T-Rex fight a Spinosaurus and all would be well in her world.

I must have watched all of the Jurassic Park films but still jump, scream and hide behind her whilst she laughs maniacally at me. She has the face of an angel but the heart of a monster.

I thought it would be a phase similar to that phase her brother went through when he wanted to be Australian, but her love of the dinosaur is still going strong.

We have bought her many dinosaur gifts, replica T-Rex claws, fossilised dino poo, Spinosaurus teeth and books galore. We have taken her to dinosaur filled places, Knebworth House Gardens, Paradise Wildlife Park, the

Natural History Museum to name all of the places we have taken her.

But. Nothing would prepare us for what came next.

One day, whilst scrolling Facebook, I saw an advert for a travelling dinosaur show. Forty or so dinosaurs would be wandering the UK for a specific time only. Obviously, we had to have tickets for that so tickets I promptly bought.

The excitement in the car was fizzing. Well, the girls were excited, the boys were just there. One had to come because he was the designated driver, and the other was dragged against his will. He was a teenager and no lover of the dinosaur, but we promised him a trip to a cafe which is always a win.

The dinosaurs were animatronic, they would move and roar and be epic. Or so we thought.

The dinosaurs were so dreadful that we all had the best time. Few of the names matched the faces so my daughter, the expert, spent much of the day shouting "that's not a Spinosaurus, that's a Brachiosaurus!" or "this one has only got one eye."

There were dinosaurs that were missing teeth, one had lost a limb but all were excellent. The huge T-Rex was genuinely awesome. How they managed to get that gargantuan beast to move its animatronic head is beyond me.

We took William to a cafe and we laughed so hard at the absurdity of it all.

These dinosaurs had once been part of something impressive, I think.

Had they been on display somewhere and now they were homeless, so the plan was to tour them around Europe? Or was this their purpose in life, to travel? We found a gaggle of half dinosaurs in a pen covered with a tarpaulin sheet. Perhaps the organisers just couldn't find the energy to erect the sabre-toothed tiger? What had died first? The woolly mammoth or the will to continue of the folks in charge?

On the way back to the car we met a family who were livid. They too had a young expert who complained that "everything was wrong." They were going to write to the organisers to express their disgust at the cost of the tickets and the state they'd found the dinosaurs in.

We all nodded. Yes, it was terrible. Blah. Blah. Blah.

It wasn't terrible. It was marvellous. The dinosaurs were massive and noisy.

So what if the names were in the wrong places, who cares? We weren't there to get an education, we were there to be amused and amused we were. So what if they were missing parts, most of them had all their arms and legs and the missing teeth were probably an accurate representation as there were no dentists back then. The chocolate covered waffles were delicious and the weather was great for April, what's not to love?

When life gives you broken dinosaurs, make lemonade or something.

May 21st, 2020

Bought a present for Hattie, T-Rex poo. "Eww, I thought it was a bone!" she giggled. Nope. T-Rex bones are worth too much money, we are 'poo' level wealthy.

Pollution

Well this is a cheery one.

Why on earth would they tell me to write about pollution? I can only assume one of them was learning about it at school. This list is a few years old now, I should ask them for a new one but that would mean admitting defeat and if there's one thing a parent should never do it's give up. No, instead it's far easier to just take forever until the kids forget all about it, which is exactly what I discovered happened during a conversation with my son last night.

Anyhow. Onwards and upwards and all that.

I don't know much about pollution other than that it's bad and out of control.

I'll have a Google...

> Pollution is the introduction of harmful materials into the environment.

Oh...

There are various types apparently.

Air - gasses, fumes, coal fuelled power plants and fumes from chemical products.

Water - industrial waste, fuel spillages and poo.

Soil - industrial dumping, land development, pesticides and fertilizers.

> Noise - unwanted or disturbing sound that affects the health and wellbeing of humans and other organisms.
>
> Radioactive - radioactive substances where their presence is unwanted.
>
> Light pollution - unwanted, inappropriate or excessive artificial lighting.
>
> Thermal pollution - rise or drop in temperature in a body of water caused by humans.

Well that's depressing.

I read about fish being found full of antidepressants, oil gumming up the feathers of birds and I saw pictures of sea turtles with plastic wrapped around their necks. Well that's no longer just depressing, it's horrific and unnecessary.

I have noticed a connection between all of the above... it's us isn't it?

Pollution is bad. Do not pollute. Recycle what you can. Walk when possible.

Be a Womble, never drop your litter or dump your unwanted crap at the side of the road.

Be kind to our beautiful planet, it's the only one we have. Well, until we colonize Mars.

To recap; keep your rubbish to yourself, reuse, repurpose and remember, be it overground or underground, womble free.

June 9th, 2015

"Mum, I've been sick in your bed!"

Of course you have, only a fool would be sick in their own bed.

Children

To have or not to have, that is a question

I never wanted children because they do nothing but vomit and they cost a fortune yet something in me stirred at around 35. For reasons unknown I decided that, if I was to have children, I'd best get on with it.

My son arrived a year later, not so closely followed by my daughter, and I'm happy to report that children don't vomit as much as you would think. They do cost a fortune though. They are fed and dressed and happy, I hope, but we have threadbare carpets, a hole in the living room floor and every room needs decorating. Hey ho. We'll have a posh house one day and I'll be as miserable as a miserable thing.

Anyhow.

Reasons to go ahead and have children...

Jam sandwiches. When and why do we stop eating jam sandwiches?

Swings. You get to take your offspring to the park where you can ignore them and have a go on the swings. They are as much fun now as they always were.

Sandcastles. No explanation necessary.

Rice crispy cakes. Easy to make and delicious.

Christmas. I've never not been excited about Christmas, I still believe and I'm 54 years young, but children make it all the more magical.*

Fun. They're hilarious, mostly when they're not trying to be.

Love. They love you unconditionally, right up until about 13 when they realise, you're just a human and you're winging it as much as they are but with bills. Enjoy the adoration whilst it lasts.

In house technical support. They're really handy to have around when you need technical help because they're newer than you, they are up to date on all things computer, smart phone/smart tv and air fryer related. It'll be back to the dark ages for me when they fly the nest.

Reasons not to have children...

Money. You can kiss goodbye to your hard earned.

Worry. Oh the never ending worry. Do they eat enough veg? Are they getting enough exercise? Do they spend too much time staring at a screen? Will they ever get a job or be able to afford a home? Will the world around them ever calm the fuck down?

Because you don't want to.

*only kidding, they ruin Christmas, it's much more fun now they know

December 4th, 2015

Just arrived at Nanny's to pick my children up and take them home. I have missed them so.

One glanced in my general direction and groaned. The other said, "I want to stay, I might cry so I can never go home."

Feeling the love tonight. Pair of arses.

Halloween

My son hated/hates Halloween. We only took him the once and it wasn't his cup of cocoa. My daughter on the other hand, oh she loves it.

I'm not sure how old she was when we first went trick or treating, 7 or 8 ish. We went with a gaggle of her friends, all dressed up as something horrific when they could have just wandered the village as themselves. They were feral, the lot of them.

Mostly boys, they were her crew at school, and my daughter running amok. It was horrific. My little princess, or "the twin boys" as my auntie Lynn liked to call her, had always been loud but this was next level noise. The knocking on doors, the raucous laughter, the hollering and screaming. I hated it. Utter chaos in small human form but to her it was the, "best time ever!"

We went again the following year but then along came covid so in 2020 we had a Halloween themed party at home. I baked a cake and covered it with eyes. I fashioned a sausage plait and gave it eyes to look mummified. So basically, I just made regular food with eyes. Then we all had to dress up using things found around the house. It was lovely.

My son threw a white towel over his head. Job jobbed. It was more than we expected of him to be fair.

The following year the little horrors were off again. It was like *The Purge* but noisier.

I had always thought it was the sweets that did it. Being handed a barrel load of sugar when you're usually restricted must be heaven but no, as time went on I realised that she's not that into sweets, she's a pastry lover, pastry and

Yorkshire puddings, neither of which are usually given out on Halloween.

What she loves about Halloween is Halloween. Blood and guts, the costumes and the screaming.

So, now that she's finally too old for hammering on people's doors for sweets she won't eat, we decided to take her to a Halloween event, one with actors and staging of all things horrible.

I was terrified, this was my idea of hell but not in a good way. I felt sick as we waited for our time slot. My daughter found my discomfort absolutely hilarious.

A man dressed as something horrible arrived to tell us the rules of the evening. No taking of photos and no touching the actors. So, I thought to myself, if I can't touch them then they, sure as hell is hot, can't touch me. What a game changer, I couldn't have given less of a fig, the nerves vanished and I was ready to watch my teenager have the time of her life.

At one point she almost threw up, I had to stand her in a corner with my back to God alone knew what and get her to breathe slowly until the urge to vomit over the dead bride subsided. It was then I who found it all hilarious.

It was so good, the actors were amazing, including the one who crept up behind me and whispered sweet hideousness's in my ear, he was just fabulous. I didn't even run when the chap with the chainsaw was chasing us, so confident was I that I was the safest I'd ever been. The irony is that, on a daily basis, I am anxious as an anxious thing yet here I was, surrounded by the macabre, feeling cool as a popsicle.

After many twists and turns around the old house we came to what looked like your average hospital ward but with more severed limbs than you would usually encounter. There was a man telling us a story but all I could hear was, "can we go back?"

My daughter had gone again, white as the many ghosts we'd passed, she felt hot and sick and needed to escape. Again I'm facing her, my back to the action, telling her that we couldn't, we were too far in now and I didn't know the way. It was at this point the blood covered surgeon made his way towards us. I'm preparing to get between him and my daughter lest we saw her dinner again, but he was heading past us to open the door. The door led us outside to hot chocolate, toasted marshmallows, axe throwing and fresh air.

I'd had a blast. I turned to my pale, weirdly quiet, daughter expecting her to refuse to ever do anything like that ever again.

"Did you enjoy that?"

"Hell yeah! Can we go again?"

October 31st 2021

I keep being asked about Halloween. Will trick or treating be a thing this year? Or will covid cancel it?

If you'd like me to be happy the answer is no. If you prefer Hattie then the answer is yes.

Computers

Not a clue

Well, I know nothing about computers. They're handy I suppose, when they are working but, when they're not... well, we cease to function.

You must have been on the phone to someone, insurance company or the doctor's surgery, and they've asked you to bear with them as their computer had "gone down."

So, are computers good or bad?

From what I can remember we did ok without them.

As I write I remember Alan Turin and his computer, the Bombe, that helped us win a war, so I've just broken my own argument, computers are good.

But, computers can be hacked so they must be bad.

Ah, but can they be hacked more than say... the postal system? I was once offered an unsigned credit card by a postie. He would simply just not deliver them and would sell them for £50 a pop. I politely declined. He was caught eventually and sacked on the spot but still, bit of an eye opener.

For the record, this was not a postie at my office. The naughtiest thing any of us ever did was try one of The Commander's cocktails one Christmas and leave the office feeling a bit happy. It made a chilly winter delivery a much jollier experience. Can recommend. I shouldn't but I do.

So. Computers, good or bad?

Now that we all carry one in our pockets, I suppose we are sunk either way. We can pay bills whilst waiting for a train, read a book or watch the telly whilst queueing at the supermarket which is all great. But we can also lose hours to social media watching short clips of animals doing crazy things. I wouldn't mind so much but you can watch 30 videos and only one or two of those will be hilarious. It's a time sucking exercise that annoys and delights me all at once.

Then there's the reaction videos. What the fudge is that about?

The left of your screen is a video of something, cooking perhaps or someone being wise from the front seat of their car, and the right of your screen has some numpty nodding away like an eejit. When did you ever see a person sitting on the bus, head in a good book, and the passenger next to them nodding their approval?

My daughter has just appeared stage left and asked Alexa to play Sir Mixalot, apparently, it's good writing music. Now, is Alexa a computer? If so, then computers are great. I didn't want an Alexa in the house, but The Husband bought one anyway and now I couldn't live without her. I only ask her to play music. I'm sure she's capable of much more but I'm just happy to hear songs that I've long forgotten about.

The upshot of all this is that I still know nothing worth knowing.

There are pros and cons as with everything that ever there were.

If someone took my phone away, would I curl up and die? No. Would I get stuff done? Yes, probably. Would I miss out? Yes.

You've all seen that wee cockatoo dancing to Elvis? It's on YouTube. He tries to get his friend to join in but he's having none of it. When the world gives you lemons chuck them in the bin and watch the Elvis loving cockatoo. The only reason to carry a computer in your pocket.

Good or bad? Not a clue. AI on the other hand... what the fuck?!!!

My dad.

Kind. Funny. Generous. Perhaps too generous. This man was never going to be rich because he gave so much away. He gave my first car away to one of his employees who couldn't get to work when their car died. This sounds worse than it should. I hadn't passed my test yet and I'd get another car. Although … it was an orange Talbot Sunbeam so perhaps it is as terrible as it sounds.

He'd once fallen onto his head from a great height, lucky to live to be honest but he did lose the ability to smell or taste anything. If he ate something he'd eaten before the accident then he could taste it but if it was something new then he couldn't. We tested him with cola and milk bottle sweets. He 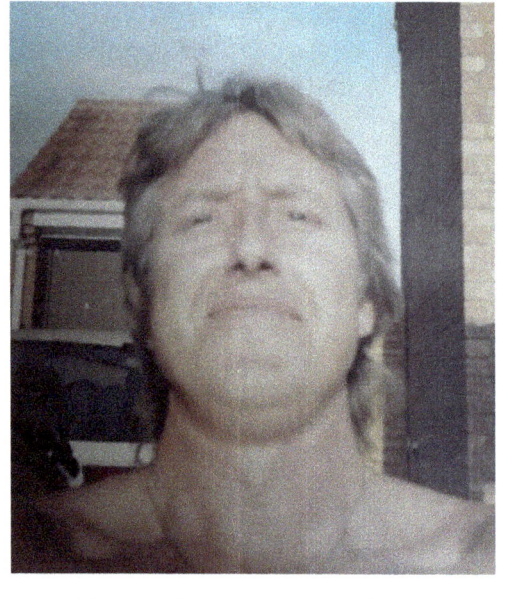 closed his eyes then we'd pop in a sweet and wait. He couldn't tell the difference. Not sure why this is the first thing to spring to my mind, I have many other stories but there you go.

We lost him in 2019 but, if I allow myself to think about him, it still feels like yesterday was the day we said goodbye.

Absolutely fucking heartbreaking, so we pretend he's gone to Australia with Auntie Lynn, Uncle David and our grandparents. They're all on the beach, looking out over the ocean, waiting for the rest of us. We're in no hurry but it will be lovely when we do get to see them all again.

www.ingramcontent.com/pod-product-compliance
Lightning Source LLC
Chambersburg PA
CBHW071721040426
42446CB00011B/2154